Global Cities
LONDON

Paul Mason
Photographs by Rob Bowden and Adrian Cooper

CHELSEA HOUSE
PUBLISHERS
An imprint of Infobase Publishing

London

Copyright 2006 © by Evans Brothers Limited

Chelsea House
An imprint of Infobase Publishing
132 West 31st Street
New York NY 10001

Library of Congress Cataloging-in-Publication Data
Mason, Paul, 1967-
    London / Paul Mason ; photographs by Rob Bowden.
        p. cm. -- (Global cities)
    "First published by Evans Brothers Limited"--T.p. verso.
    Includes index.
    ISBN 0-7910-8852-9 (acid-free paper)
    1. London (England)--Juvenile literature. I. Bowden, Rob. II. Title. III. Series.
    DA677.M37 2006
    942.1--dc22   2006045457

Printed in China.

10 9 8 7 6 5 4 3 2 1

This book is printed on acid-free paper.
Designer: Robert Walster, Big Blu Design
Maps and graphics: Martin Darlinson

All photographs are by Rob Bowden (EASI-Images) except the following:
by Adrian Cooper (EASI-Images), 11 top, 15 top, 17, 19, 20, 21, 23, 24 top,
25 top, 27, 28 bottom, 29 bottom, 31 bottom, 34 top, 35 bottom, 37, 38 top,
40 top, 42, 43 top, 51 bottom left, 51 bottom right, 52 bottom, 53, 54 bottom, 55 top;
by Corbis/Bettmann, 12 bottom; by Corbis, 15 bottom;
by Edward Parker (EASI-Images), 16, 18 bottom, 25 bottom;
courtesy Great Ormond Street Hospital, 29 top;
by Paul Mason, 43 bottom.

First published by Evans Brothers Limited
2A Portman Mansions, Chiltern Street, London W1U 6NR, United Kingdom
This edition published under license from Evans Brothers Limited. All rights reserved.

Contents

An urban world

As of 2007 the world's population will, for the first time in history, be more urban than rural. An estimated 3.3 billion people will find themselves living in towns and cities such as London, and for many, the experience of urban living will be relatively new. For example, in China, the world's most populous country, the number of people living in urban areas increased from 196 million in 1980 to more than 536 million in 2005.

The urban challenge...

This staggering rate of urbanization (the process by which a country's population becomes concentrated into towns and cities) is being repeated around much of the world and presents the world with a complex set of challenges for the 21st century. Many of these challenges are local, like the provision of clean water for expanding urban populations, but others are global in scale. In 2003 an outbreak of the highly contagious disease SARS demonstrated this as it spread rapidly among the populations of well-connected cities around the globe. The pollution generated by urban areas is also a global concern, particularly because urban residents tend to generate more than their rural counterparts.

▼ London in relation to southern England and (inset) neighboring countries.

... and opportunity!

Urban centers, and particularly major cities such as London, also provide great opportunities for improving life at both a local and global scale. Cities concentrate people and allow for efficient forms of mass transportation such as subway or light rail networks. Services too, such as waste collection, recycling, education, and health care, can all function more efficiently in a city. Cities are centers of learning and often the birthplace of new ideas, from innovations in science and technology to new ways of day-to-day living. Cities also provide a platform for the celebration of arts and culture, and as their populations become more multicultural such celebrations are increasingly global in their reach.

▲ The River Thames winds through the city of London, here passing the financial district.

London facts

Population: more than 7.6 million in 2005

Population density: 11,844 people per square mile

Area, Greater London: 612 square miles

Parks/green spaces: 147 plus 8 royal parks, 30 percent of area

Communities: more than 50 nonnative communities of more than 10,000 people

A trading center

From its very beginnings as a settlement 2,000 years ago, London has been a trading center. Today it is the richest city in Europe, employing more than 3.5 million people—nearly 6 percent of the entire population of the United Kingdom. People come to London because pay is better than elsewhere in the country (an average of 20 percent higher) and there are more job opportunities. Living costs are also greater, however.

A big part of London's success is due to the City of London, which is home to the London Stock Exchange and many globally important financial institutions. "The City," as it is known, is part of London but separate from it, governed by its own rules and regulations and with its own police force. The City's financial influence spreads around the globe: It is the world's biggest center for international lending, bond trading, and foreign exchange trading.

▼ The famous "Gherkin" building of the insurance company Swiss Re, one of the financial institutions that have chosen to locate in the City of London.

▼ Central London, with its major roads.

A global melting pot

Many of the world's different nationalities are represented among London's people. People from Commonwealth countries (which were once under British rule) such as Bangladesh, India, Nigeria, South Africa, Jamaica, and Australia have all moved to London to live and work. There are also significant communities of Poles, Turks, Colombians, Argentines, and many others.

▶ Members of the long-established Bangladeshi community in Brick Lane, one of London's most famous ethnic communities.

Rich and poor

One division in London life is financial, rather than geographical. Areas such as Kensington and Chelsea are home to some of the world's richest people, but close by may be social housing for people that are much less affluent.

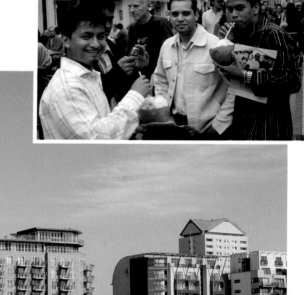

▲ New luxury developments in the once working-class Docklands are blurring divides within London.

Dividing London

Greater London occupies an area of 612 square miles. Londoners cope with the size of their city by mentally dividing it into smaller areas. The first division is north or south of the River Thames: People think of themselves as North or South Londoners. Within these two large areas are many smaller ones, such as Hackney in the north or Brixton in the south. Londoners also think of themselves in terms of east and west. "Out west" are areas such as Twickenham and Ealing. To the east are the areas where poor manual workers once lived, such as Whitechapel and Bow—the homes of "Cockneys." A true Cockney is said to be someone born within hearing range of the bells of St. Mary le Bow, a church in the City of London.

The history of London

London began life as a Roman settlement in the mid-first century, and at one time it was capital of Roman Britain. Despite being abandoned by the Romans in 415, London continued to grow. In 730, the English historian Bede wrote that it was "the mart [market] of many nations resorting [traveling] to it by land and sea." In 1016 London became capital of England. By 1066 King Edward the Confessor had completed the building work on London's famous Westminster Abbey.

Medieval London

Between 1348 and 1375 there were several waves of the "Black Death," a plague that had already swept across the rest of Europe. In the cramped, unhygienic city, plague spread like wildfire. It killed roughly two thirds of the city's population of 75,000 people.

The Catholic Church came to own many of London's main buildings, but in 1536 King Henry VIII announced the dissolution of the monasteries. Lands and property owned by the Catholic Church were sold off. Private owners, mainly nobles, bought the properties, changing the ownership of the city center forever.

▲ One the few medieval buildings remaining in the heart of London.

▼ The plague struck rich and poor, young and old. Houses with dead were marked with a cross.

▼ The Globe Theatre was originally built in 1599. Today many plays from the 1600s are staged at this reconstructed version.

London first became a truly global city under Queen Elizabeth I. Britain's merchant fleets brought goods to the city, and in 1572 the Royal Exchange was built, where goods from around the world could be traded. Elizabeth's reign was also the time of great playwrights such as William Shakespeare. Today Londoners can spend an evening at the rebuilt Globe Theatre, where many of Shakespeare's plays are now performed, just as they were when they were first written.

Civil War

London played a crucial role in the English Civil War (1642–45), fought between the supporters of King Charles I and Parliamentary forces demanding greater freedom to make laws. In 1642 Charles had a chance to capture the city but 24,000 Londoners turned out to defend it. Charles withdrew and missed his chance of victory. He was executed in London's Whitehall almost seven years later, in 1649.

Restoration and the plague

By 1660, Londoners had had enough of the closed theaters and other harsh laws brought in by the ruling Parliamentarians after the Civil War. Londoners welcomed the restoration of the monarchy and the new king, Charles II, with open arms. He repaid them by immediately ordering the theaters to reopen, and plays were soon being performed again.

In 1665 the city was again hit by plague. London was, as always, densely packed with people, and that summer's hot weather meant the disease spread quickly. Dogs and cats were thought to carry the plague, so all were killed. This led to an explosion in London's rat population, because there were now no dogs or cats to kill rats. Since rats were the true carriers of the fleas that spread the plague to humans, the effect was disastrous, with thousands dying daily.

The Great Fire

The plague died down over winter, but the next year, 1666, Londoners had to deal with an immense fire. On September 2 a fire that started in a bakery caused almost 80 percent of the city to burn to the ground. The fire leapt from building to building in London's narrow streets, and the old timber-framed houses quickly went up in smoke. Very few people died, but more than 100,000 people lost their homes.

In the aftermath of the Great Fire, London was rebuilt to include many of the landmark buildings that are found in the city today. Architects such as Sir Christopher Wren laid out new squares and crescents of houses and rebuilt almost all the city's churches, among them St. Paul's Cathedral (right). In just five years 90,000 new homes were built.

The 1700s and 1800s

Throughout the 1700s, London continued to grow. By now it was the largest city in the world, with a population of almost a million. The growth of the city posed problems for the authorities, as London was rapidly becoming a lawless place. People carried so many weapons that the writer Horace Walpole said people were "forced to travel even at noon as if . . . going into battle." The problem was only contained when the world's first official police force was founded in 1829.

Meanwhile, trade and industry continued to increase as Britain's empire grew. The docks unloaded increasing amounts of goods from around the world: cotton from India, sugar from Jamaica, wool from Australia, and much else besides. By 1901 more than 7 million people were said to be living in London, often crowded into very unhealthy living conditions. Measles, whooping cough, cholera, and scarlet fever killed thousands of residents, rich and poor, in the 18th and 19th centuries.

▲ St. Paul's Cathedral is the most famous building in London to arise from the ashes of the Great Fire.

▼ St. Katharine Docks, once important for trade in the city, has now being converted into dockside homes, stores, and restaurants.

Westminster Abbey

Westminster Abbey has played a central role in the history of London and the nation since it was consecrated in 1065. The coronation of every monarch since William the Conqueror in 1066 (with the exceptions of the Edward V and Edward VIII, who were never crowned) has taken place in the Abbey. It contains the tombs of kings and queens, and the graves and memorials to the great and good of the nation, including statesmen, writers, scientists, artists, and musicians. More than 3,000 people are buried there.

The Abbey was rebuilt in the middle of the 13th century, when King Henry III (1216–72) decided to rebuild it in the current Gothic style of architecture. He wanted the Abbey to be not only a place of worship, but also a place for the coronation and burial of monarchs. The Abbey has a large collection of monumental sculpture, including the tomb of the Unknown Warrior.

▲ The west face of Westminster Abbey.

In 1965 the Abbey celebrated its 900th anniversary, with the theme "One People." The theme aimed to reflect the Abbey's long involvement with the life of the British people. Today, as well as holding regular services of worship, it hosts special services to mark great events in the life of the nation—such as the funeral of the Queen Mother, Elizabeth, the mother of Queen Elizabeth II.

◄ The state funeral of Elizabeth, the Queen Mother, held in the Abbey in 2002.

15

▲ The first half of the 20th century saw the construction of large suburban areas on the outskirts of the city. Houses with adequate living space for the average family started to become more affordable.

The 20th century

As the 20th century dawned, London was a divided city. The rich lived very well indeed. Britain was the wealthiest country in the world, and London its richest city. Luxury hotels such as the Ritz and expensive department stores such as Harrods grew up at this time.

London's poor still lived in very harsh conditions, though after several strikes by unskilled workers in the late 19th century, things were slowly improving. Gas, water, electricity, and transportation for the city were slowly being brought into public ownership; the London County Council (LCC) had begun to buy up these utilities on behalf of the people of the city. One problem all Londoners still had to contend with was the city's famous "pea soupers"—

incredibly thick fogs, caused partly by terrible air pollution from nearby factories. After the end of the First World War in 1918, some Londoners began to move to the suburbs. Over the next 20 years they moved to places such as Dagenham in the east, one of the LCC's new communities.

The Blitz

During the Second World War (1939–45), the German air force tried to bomb the United Kingdom into submission by attacking London in a series of air raids between September 1940 and May 1941. The raids became known as the Blitz, and they destroyed large areas of the city. By the end, more than 30,000 people had died and 130,000 buildings been destroyed.

Postwar London

By the end of the Second World War, more than 80 percent of London's houses had been damaged in some way by bombing. Partly because of this, more people began to move away from the city, and the population shrank for the first time since the Romans left in 415.

To replace bombed houses, the LCC began a program of building huge public housing projects, known as estates. To replace departed workers, and those who had died in the war, in the 1950s the government began to recruit workers from Caribbean colonies. People from Trinidad, Jamaica, and other islands started to arrive in London for the first time.

During the 1960s the LCC was replaced by the Greater London Council (GLC), which had authority over a much bigger area. By the 1980s the GLC was proposing radical solutions to some of London's problems. These included a subsidized public transportation policy, which made buses and trains so cheap that thousands of Londoners stopped using their cars.

The GLC's radical approach was unpopular with the right-wing government of Prime Minister Margaret Thatcher, and in 1986 the GLC was abolished. As a result, the city had no representative government of its own until the formation of a Greater London Assembly and the election of a Mayor of London in 2000.

▲ During the 1960s, building large apartment towers like this was seen as a good way of providing inexpensive homes for large numbers of Londoners.

◀ Immigrants from Asia and the Caribbean began to arrive in London from the 1950s onward.

The people of London

London is one of the most ethnically diverse cities in Europe. More than 300 different languages are spoken within the city's boundaries, and it has citizens with family origins from all over the world.

▲ London's many mosques are key meeting places for the city's Muslim communities.

London communities

Londoners from different backgrounds can live in a far more integrated way than people in many other similar cities. Even so, immigrant communities are sometimes associated with particular areas, for instance, the Indian Gujeratis in Wembley and Afro-Caribbeans in Brixton.

Today more than 30 percent of London's population are either first-, second-, or third-generation immigrants. These are people whose families arrived in London after the Second World War, coming from the Caribbean or the Indian subcontinent (India, Pakistan, and Bangladesh). Today, London's new immigrants are more likely to be fleeing the world's wars, and to come from Somalia, Bosnia, Iran, or Iraq.

◄ Since 1964, Notting Hill has held a carnival during August. The carnival was originally led by Trinidadian immigrants, but today is a multicultural event.

Juliano and Talita

Brazilians Juliano and Talita share a one-bedroom apartment with another couple and their young daughter in Harlesden, a part of London with a growing community of Brazilians and Portuguese. Juliano works as a motorcycle courier, despite having trained to be a pharmacist in Brazil. Talita works as a cleaner; she studied sports science in college. Juliano's father is Italian, which means he can have an Italian passport. Because Italy is part of the European Union, Juliano can work in the United Kingdom.

Juliano first came to the UK in 1999 to earn money to pay for college. He worked as a bartender, hotel cleaner, and at various other odd jobs. He returned to Brazil for four years and earned his pharmacy degree. He met Talita in Brazil, at college. After graduation they came back to London together. Juliano says, "I told Talita, I know every place, trust me . . . but after six months I thought it was a complete mistake. Everything seemed to go wrong. My motorcycle broke, then it got stolen, all in my first week of work. I almost wanted to go back. Talita said to me, 'Let's stay; we made the effort to come here.'"

Juliano could adapt his Brazilian degree and get work in a pharmacy in London, but with little English and a loose grasp of how the city works, it is difficult to find out how. He relies on word-of-mouth among fellow Brazilians more than anything. Also, there's hardly enough time to find out because his job takes up too much of his time.

Some immigrants to London have made a shorter, less perilous journey to reach the city. These are people drawn to the city by its facilities, good wages, and other attractions. They come from all over Britain and mainland Europe, particularly the new member states of the European Union (EU).

Alongside the immigrant communities are "native" Londoners: those whose grandparents and parents weren't tempted to move out to the suburbs.

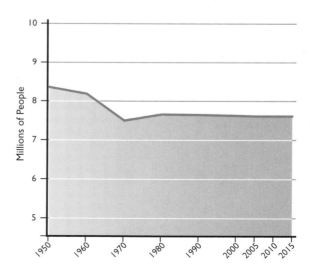

▶ London population movements, 1950–2015. The city's population level is not expected to fluctuate in the forseeable future.

Population issues

London is one of Europe's largest cities; in 2005 only Paris and Moscow had bigger populations. With a population of well over 7 million, London has more inhabitants than many countries, including Israel, Denmark, and Norway.

In 1950 London was the third-largest city in the world, but by 2015 it will no longer even make the top 30, as other cities of global importance continue to expand in population. In addition to this change, over the last 50 years London's population has slowly been shrinking. Even the large numbers of new citizens arriving from abroad and elsewhere in the United Kingdom cannot keep pace with the numbers of people leaving.

In recent years the trend of people leaving the city has been accelerated by the increase in property values. Many Londoners, like British people generally, own their own homes. Someone who bought a house for £100,000 in 1980 might find it worth more than £1 million (about $1.74 million) today. Property prices are lower outside the capital, so some Londoners have left, using the money they made to start a new life elsewhere.

▲ London's large population generates huge amounts of waste daily.

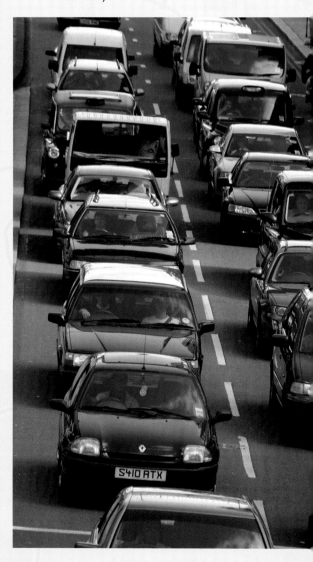

▶ London's roads are always busy, especially when people are trying to get to or from work or leaving the city for the weekend.

A crowded city

Today London's population is stable at around 7.6 million people, who live in an area of 612 square miles. Because 30 percent of London is made up of parks and green space, the area actually available for housing and businesses is far smaller than this. Londoners are used to being jammed into tight spaces: in line, on sidewalks, and traveling on the city's underground "Tube" trains, for example.

The size of London's population raises a wide variety of challenges for the city's planners. Many Londoners are living inside the boundaries of a city originally laid out to fit far fewer people, moving more slowly. The city's infrastructure (for example, the road, transportation, power, and water systems, and the other things that make it possible to live in a modern city) dates originally from well over 100 years ago.

▲ During the morning and evening rush, public transportation, like this Tube train, can be very crowded.

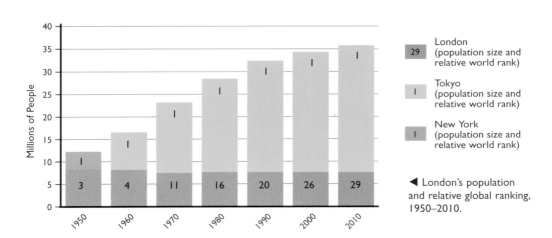

London
29 (population size and relative world rank)

Tokyo
1 (population size and relative world rank)

New York
1 (population size and relative world rank)

◀ London's population and relative global ranking, 1950–2010.

Pressures

Today, a Londoner from 1900 would find the layout of central London familiar. The biggest difference would be that cars, buses, bicycles, and motorbikes use the familiar streets of Victorian London, rather than horse-drawn carriages. Each day millions of pollution-creating cars and other vehicles take to the city's roads.

Other issues are less visible, but no less important: The same Victorian sewer system now carries the wastewater of millions: from toilets, washing machines, dishwashers, showers, and other modern appliances; tons of trash have to be disposed of every day; power and water have to be supplied to millions of homes and businesses; housing, schools, and hospitals are all needed. All these issues are crucial if the city is to be a viable place for people to live in the future.

▲ Concern about crime is one of the things people dislike about living in London. London's police force, the Metropolitan Police, tries to be highly visible as a way of reassuring people.

Conflicts and crime

Racial and cultural conflicts are not new in London, though historically Londoners have been more likely to stage a riot against the authorities than against other Londoners, wherever they are from. Nonetheless, conflicts between different ethnic groups of Londoners exist. In some parts of London political parties have fanned the flames of these conflicts as a way of winning votes.

Crime is a concern for Londoners, with muggings and burglaries at the top of the list. Often these are linked to other problems such as alcohol and drug abuse. People with no job or money pay for their addictions by breaking into houses and apartments to steal goods, which they then sell for a fraction of their true worth.

Language challenge

London has large numbers of first-generation immigrants for whom English is not a first language. In some London schools there are more Punjabi speakers, for example, than English speakers. The government wants new citizens to adapt to British values, and the first step for many immigrant children is to learn English.

Homelessness

Homelessness is a problem in London, with whole communities of people living on the streets, under bridges, or in abandoned buildings. Some have come to the city from elsewhere in the hope of a good life and instead found it impossible to get a place to live or a job. Among the homeless are also people with mental health problems, runaways, alcoholics, and drug addicts.

◄ This man is selling the *Big Issue*, a weekly paper sold by homeless people as a way of earning money.

CASE STUDY

Edwin, Crisis volunteer

Born in 1944, Edwin came to London as a soldier in the Royal Scots Dragoon Guards. In 1972 he had a number-one hit single, "Amazing Grace," with his regimental band. At the same time he started drinking heavily. He was thrown out of the army, and 34 years of homelessness and substance abuse followed.

In 2005 he moved into a home, in Uxbridge. "I had a dream of a Rolls-Royce and golden streets, but it wasn't to be. There was no gold." He no longer drinks and has become a volunteer for Crisis, a charity that helps homeless people improve their lives, giving art and craft classes. He also gives advice to young homeless people. "When you're on the streets you see all walks of life. People's marriages break down, people lose their jobs, mental health, bankruptcy . . . there's all sorts of reasons why people are on street corners. Main thing is we're all human beings. You have to fend for yourself and keep your head looking out, watching your back all the time. I'm one of two survivors out of a group of 15 people I used to hang around with. The rest have died from alcohol. London has changed. There are more young people on the streets. More fighting, too. It's more dangerous now than 20 years ago. Street people are stealing and robbing from one another, and that never used to happen. They can't trust each other. Now I come home and put on some CDs, do some cooking. It's hard to get used to paying the rent on time, buying food for yourself, and cooking. But, of course, it's worth it."

23

Living in the city

Perhaps the most pressing problem London faces is creating enough affordable housing. Housing costs have risen steeply over the last 50 years. As wages have risen in the better-paid industries such as banking and law, house prices and rents have risen as well. As a result, workers in essential services, such as nursing, cannot afford homes.

Types of housing

London contains a wide variety of housing. In the center, where space is precious, most homes are apartments, or "flats," often created by dividing up large old houses. Farther from the middle of the city, houses become more common. Farther out still, people's houses might even be semidetached, with a garage and a yard.

The city's public housing is scattered throughout London, known as "council estates" or just "estates." Many of these are high-rise apartment towers, originally designed to house low-paid workers. People are able to rent these homes from the local government for an affordable rent, provided that there are enough to go around. In the 1980s the national government introduced laws that allowed

▲ In recent years, many older buildings have been demolished to make way for new homes.

people to buy their rented council homes at low prices. Many took advantage of the offer, and today some former council flats are privately owned and unavailable for poorer residents.

▼ Historic properties with character, like these Georgian period houses in north London, can sell for very high prices.

Essential workers

Few of London's essential workers, such as nurses, teachers, firefighters, and ambulance drivers, earn enough to buy a home. To provide them with housing, housing associations may offer them an affordable way to own a share in a property. The worker buys a part share, then pays reduced rent to the association for the other share. The London Assembly is trying to make sure that when new housing developments are built, some of the homes are reserved for jobs for essential workers so that they can live near their jobs.

▶ Some of London's newly built homes are set aside for "key" or "essential" worker—teachers and nurses, for example.

Parks and gardens

Parks and gardens take up almost a third of London. These green spaces are important to Londoners, who put them to a wide variety of uses. On Hampstead Heath, for example, are the famous Bathing Ponds, used as swimming pools. People use the parks for exercise, including running, soccer, and horse riding, and for leisure activities such as picnics. They are also important as an escape from the hustle of city life, for breathing some fresh air and relaxing outdoors.

▼ Enjoying St. James's Park, one of the large parks in the center of the city.

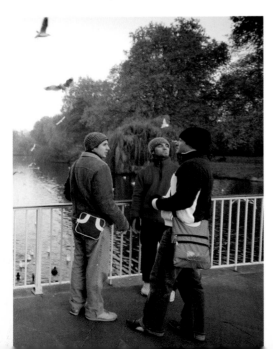

▼ Average temperatures and rainfall for London.

▲ High-fashion stores are found in areas such as Old Bond Street, Covent Garden, and Knightsbridge.

Shopping

London is famous as a center for fashion designers. In Covent Garden and on Old Bond Street are stores selling clothes from designers such as Paul Smith, Stella McCartney, and Alexander McQueen. Most Londoners buy their clothes at the less expensive stores that are found everywhere in the city. Clothes are also an important part of the city's outdoor markets, where everything from a new pair of socks to an antique ball gown can be purchased.

Food

Each area of London once had at least a weekly food market, and many were held every day. Since the Second World War may of these markets have closed due to competition from supermarkets, but in several parts of London they remain a thriving part of the community.

Among the most famous are London's traditional old wholesale markets, such as the Smithfield meat market, which has been in existence since 1327. Produce from the countryside arrives at Smithfield to be sold to the butchers, greengrocers, stallholders, flower sellers, and chefs of the city. Farmers' markets are increasingly popular in London. In these, small-scale food producers bring their goods to the city to sell them directly to the people who will eat them. Many farmers' markets sell organic goods, which are becoming more popular every year.

▶ These butchers work at Smithfield meat market.

26

Maggy O'Grady

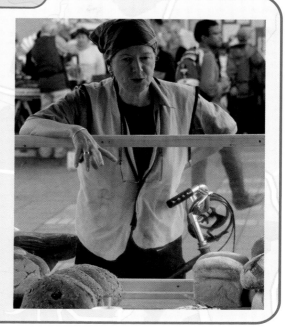

Maggy shops at the farmers' market in Peckham Square. Maggy, a Camberwell resident of 25 years, is here to buy fresh bread. Last week she bought Turk's head (a vegetable) and squashes. "As autumn and winter set in, it's about keeping the summer sunshine in my kitchen. It's more expensive to buy from farmers' markets, but I think it's worth it. Of course it's about not going to a supermarket, but it isn't just about the food. Damilola Taylor, a young boy, was murdered near here a few years ago, and for our community spirit it is important to participate in things such as local markets. It helps keep the area lively. You could say it helps dispel ghosts."

▲ London has some of the oldest markets in the world; today they are increasing in popularity once more.

Urban health issues

Londoners confront several challenges to keeping fit and healthy while living in the city. Many Londoners get up by 7:00 a.m. to have breakfast and head off to work, taking an hour or more to arrive. They have a busy, long day and get home late in the evening. They may not have the time or energy to cook a meal from fresh ingredients. Instead they rely on convenience foods, which simply have to be heated up, or ready-to-eat fast foods.

These foods have greatly increased in popularity since the 1980s, when they first appeared in London. Unfortunately, they are now linked to a number of serious health problems, including heart disease and obesity. Many children in particular are now experiencing health problems from eating too much convenience food and fast food. In 2005 a local TV chef, Jamie Oliver, helped to raise awareness about healthy eating during a campaign to persuade schools in London (and nationally) to provide more nutritious meals.

▲ Joggers are a common sight on the streets.

▼ The importance of healthy eating is now emphasized in schools.

Another issue for London residents is the amount of alcohol they consume. With so many restaurants, bars, theaters, and pubs, many Londoners find that their social lives can very easily involve drinking alcohol. Alcohol is responsible for increased levels of heart disease and liver problems, among many other health troubles.

The city's air pollution also causes health problems. An increasing proportion of children are suffering from the breathing disorder asthma, which is a potential killer. Some experts have linked this increase to increased air pollution from cars.

Hospitals and doctors

Like people in the rest of the United Kingdom, Londoners can use the free National Health Service (NHS). Few other cities of global importance are in countries with a similar health service. Anyone who is sick or injured can visit a doctor's ofice or hospital without having to pay. There is a standard fee for prescribed medicines, but people with long-term illnesses, such as diabetes, do not have to pay. There are also private hospitals and clinics, many in the area around Harley Street in Marylebone.

The city's health care system is not without its problems, however. Finding enough well-trained staff is always a problem. Stress, high living costs, and a better standard of living elsewhere mean staff can be hard to hold on to. Many employees are recruited from other countries, where the rates of pay or the living conditions may be worse than in London. Late at night, Accident and Emergency Departments (hospital emergency rooms) can sometimes be alarming places, as those who have drunk too much and hurt themselves mix with other patients.

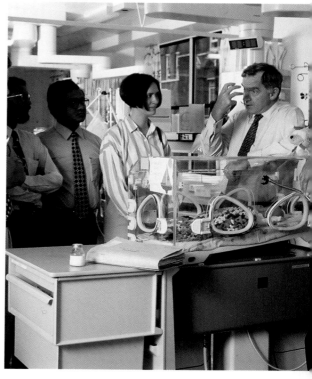

▲ Among London's medical facilities are world-famous teaching hospitals such as Great Ormond Street Hospital for Children, where pediatricians can learn new skills.

▶ Health workers at a health fair, held as part of an NHS outreach program in Southwark.

The London economy

London has an economy that contributes more than $100 billion to the UK economy. The banking and financial sector is the largest contributor to the city's economy. Other important industries include the media (television and radio companies, newspapers, and publishers), a very large retail sector, and the large law firms based in the City of London.

There is little manufacturing industry, so most Londoners work in the service sector, including the large public sector—such as the national or local government departments, of which there are many based in central London. A few workers in the financial sector can earn huge salaries, but most London workers find life less financially rewarding. Inner London is the wealthiest part of the United Kingdom, with a resilient economy that can withstand changes in economic outlook. Despite that there is still some unemployment, ranging from almost zero in the City to 13 percent in Tower Hamlets, just a ten-minute walk from the City. The high cost of traveling to work, plus higher food prices and more expensive housing than the rest of the country, means that some people struggle to make ends meet. Worst off of all are the people who work in the city center at unskilled jobs such as street sweeping or office cleaning. These jobs are low paid, but the employees' basic costs of living in the city are similar to everyone else's.

▼ Getting ready for the lunch rush at Leadenhall Market. Jobs such as waiting on tables, cleaning, and kitchen work are often poorly paid and done by recent immigrants.

Creative industries

The multiple branches of the creative and media industries are an important part of the city economy—they provide more than 400,000 jobs in London. The city also provides the infrastructure-related jobs that all big cities have, such as the transportation and construction industries and road and sewer maintenance. There are some small manufacturing businesses and an enormous retail sector.

▲ News photographers waiting outside the Houses of Parliament. The national news media are based in London and are a major employer.

CASE STUDY

Ndidi Ekubia, silversmith

Originally from Manchester, Ndidi Ekubia is a silversmith. A traditional trade, silversmithing has recently been revived and celebrated by organizations such as the Craft Council and the Jerwood Prize. Cockpit Arts, where Ndidi has worked for the last three years, is a charity that provides affordable studio space in Holborn and Deptford for designers and makers. They have an award program, called the Seedbed Award, which gives discounted rents to individuals and businesses that are just starting out.

"I work very long hours and have to support myself with a second job at the moment. Without organizations such as Cockpit it would be more difficult for designers and makers like me to survive. I work here because it's affordable, and also because I'm surrounded by other designer/makers. Silversmithing makes a lot of noise, so I need to be in the kind of environment where it is acceptable to do this kind of work. It's difficult to find affordable space like this in London. And what's good about Cockpit is they also give you business support and help with publicity and financial advice. There is also 'Open Studios' twice a year: Everybody here exhibits their work and hundreds of people from all over London come and buy our work."

The City

At the heart of London—literally and metaphorically—is the City. Physically, the City is made up of the area governed by the Corporation of London, which is the oldest local authority in England. The financial institutions that together compose the City make it one of the most powerful financial organizations in the world.

The City is sometimes called the "Square Mile" because of the compact size of its core area. Despite its tiny size, the City contributes about 3 percent of the United Kingdom's GDP and about 13 percent of London's GDP. A few facts underline the sheer amount of money that the City generates: $504 billion of foreign exchange turnover passes through the City every day; 70 percent of all Eurobonds are

▲ The Lloyd's Building, home to one of the world's biggest insurance companies, Lloyd's of London.

traded in London; $2 trillion of metal stock is traded each year in the City; and $884 billion is traded on the international futures market every day.

In 2005, 287 foreign companies were listed on the London Stock Exchange, where shares in companies are bought and sold. Many of the UK companies listed on the exchange also trade or own manufacturing facilities around the world.

▼ The London Metal Exchange, which helps regulate the world's trade in metals.

The Corporation of London

The Corporation of London provides the City with its infrastructure and runs the City of London Police (a separate force from the Metropolitan Police, who are in charge of the rest of London). The Corporation also maintains 10,000 acres of open space in and around London, including Epping Forest and Hampstead Heath. It runs three big food markets (Smithfield, Billingsgate, and Spitalfields) and provides affordable residential housing across London. The Corporation can do this because of the City's wealth and the rent it receives from its large landholdings.

Chris Giles

Chris is the Economics Editor for the *Financial Times* (or FT), a financial newspaper that began as a tip sheet and has been the most important business newspaper in London and the world for more than 100 years. Like many businesses, the FT feels it is important to keep an office in the City. "Computers mean that trading and deals can be done almost anywhere now," explains Chris, "but it is still important to be in the City. All the big global banks have an office in London and many large companies too." London's history as a financial center began with its trading past, and the square mile of "the City" was the focus for raising funds and buying and selling commodities. Chris explains that the financial sector has spread to new areas of London, such as the Docklands and the West End, where some

smaller companies have located. "The financial sector has been growing very rapidly for the past 10 years, much faster than other parts of the UK economy. I can see no slowdown in this growth, and London is still the most important place to be for business."

The Livery

The Livery is the name for a group of 107 livery guilds based in the City. These are ancient trade associations, such as the Goldsmith's Company. Many are still important to the trade they are named after; for example, the Goldsmith's Company is responsible for testing precious metals for their purity. In 1478 the Company passed a rule that all precious metals had to be brought to its hall to be marked with the correct purity. This is the origin of the word *hallmark*, meaning a mark that reveals the purity of a metal.

▶ London's Guildhall was the original home of the City's many livery guilds.

Industrial decline

After the Second World War, London's traditional industrial sites slowly became rundown. Manufacturing in the United Kingdom in general had begun to decline as the economy shifted toward a service industry base. At the same time the importance of London as a port decreased. The East End docks, which had provided employment for generations of Londoners, fell into disuse. They became abandoned and derelict— the largest inner-city "brownfield" site in Europe.

▲ Some areas of London are still home to rundown buildings once used for businesses or industry.

Redevelopment

In recent years many of London's rundown and neglected areas have been redeveloped, sometimes with the help of the UK government. The area around Greenwich was chosen as the site of the Millennium Dome, a giant "attraction" that cost about £840 million ($1.5 billion) and has yet to find a permanent use. More successfully, the Canary Wharf area was redeveloped into offices and homes on a formerly derelict site. Many businesses, particularly financial institutions, relocated to the Canary Wharf area, attracted by lower rents and new transportation links.

▼ The East End around Canary Wharf in Docklands has become a rival location to the City for global corporations.

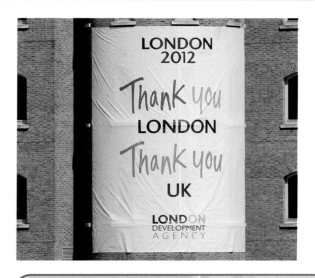

The 2012 Olympics

London's winning bid to host the 2012 Olympics will allow the regeneration of other rundown areas of the city. The transportation links and sports facilities that the Olympics will need will later be available for London's citizens, thus improving their lives. Other host cities, notably Barcelona in Spain, have used the Olympics in just this way.

◄ Signs celebrate the fact that London will host the Olympics in 2012.

CASE STUDY

Rufus Clarke

Rufus is a Neighborhood Youth Coordinator, aged 45. He's lived in Tower Hamlets all his life and been a youth worker for 15 years. "My work is about young people's futures. Tonight, for example, I've got a social enterprise project running that trains them how to build computers. And once they have built one, and pass the course with the right skills, they keep the computer. It's an incentive for them to get skills. Another example is a youth banking program where money the council would pay for things such as graffiti removal and community work, such as painting old people's homes, they pay into an account for young people. When the young people have earned credits through doing the community work they can go out and buy things. Because of the 2012 Olympics, money is likely to come to the area, directly and indirectly, so I'm encouraging the young people I work with to get some sort of skill before the Olympics come. I don't want to see young people left by the wayside. The building of Canary Wharf didn't do much for our community—the homes were too expensive for the younger generation to afford. I hope the facilities built during the Olympics will be available and accessible to all our community."

Managing London

London has been the home of first England's, and then the United Kingdom's national government since the 11th century. The UK government is centered on the Houses of Parliament at Westminster. London is governed by an elected Mayor and the London Assembly, based at City Hall, across the Thames from the Tower of London.

▲ The Houses of Parliament are home to the United Kingdom's national government.

The Mayor

The first citywide Mayor was elected in 2000, with elections subsequently held every four years. In 2000 and 2004, Ken Livingstone was elected, partly because Londoners remembered his time in charge of the Greater London Council during the 1980s. The Mayor works with the borough councils (see page 38) plus the transportation, police, fire, and development authorities to develop London-wide policies for reducing crime, improving public transportation, reducing traffic congestion, making more affordable housing available, improving poor areas and the environment, supporting tourism and economic development, and planning for London's future. The City of London has its own mayor, The Lord Mayor of London, whose role involves representing the Corporation of London and promoting the City abroad.

The Assembly

The Mayor is more powerful than the Assembly; the Assembly's main role is to act as a check for the Mayor's activities. The Assembly has to have a two-thirds majority of its 25 members to overturn one of the Mayor's policies. The Mayor's office and the London Assembly are funded in various ways. Some money comes from a share of the council tax paid to local governments by everyone who lives or has a business in the city. Most money comes as grants from the UK government.

▼ The new, futuristic City Hall, seen here with Tower Bridge in the background, is home to the Mayor's office and the London Assembly. City Hall, which opened in 2002, sits by the Thames, across the river from the Tower of London.

Voting in London

To vote in city elections voters must be living in London; be a UK, EU, or Commonwealth resident aged 18 or over; and registered to vote. Voters in mayoral elections can place two votes, a first choice and a second choice. If no one wins the election when all the first-choice votes have been counted, only the two candidates with the highest numbers of votes remain in the contest. The second-choice votes of everyone who voted for other candidates are then counted, to see which of the two remaining candidates they prefer. In this way, the winner is decided. For the Assembly, voters also have two votes. One elects a named candidate for the local area; the other goes toward a party or candidate from a citywide list.

► Town halls are where the administrative units of smaller areas of London are based.

Local government

As well as having a Mayor and the London Assembly, Londoners are represented on their 32 borough councils, which act for the city's boroughs or districts.

These are responsible for such things as trash collection, schools, road maintenance, and street lighting in their particular areas of the city. The borough councils work with the Mayor and Assembly. For example, if the Mayor develops a plan for a London-wide recycling scheme, the boroughs are the bodies that actually have to put the plan into action.

Local action

History shows that Londoners have a tradition of direct action if there is something that they aren't happy about. Some Londoners, aware of the city's problems, are not content to wait for the Mayor to put a strategy together and then for their borough council to act on the strategy. Instead they take matters into their own hands. Sometimes they start campaigns—for example, petitioning for an improvement in the standard of school lunches, or to save a local sports field from being turned into a housing estate. On other occasions they actually get together and work on programs to improve their city. Volunteering for this sort of campaign is becoming more widespread as people see the success of other programs.

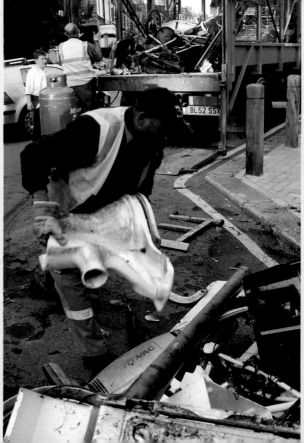

► A special pickup of illegally dumped trash. Volunteers collected the trash, and the local council worked with them to collect and dispose of it—an example of cooperation between city and residents.

Fishing the Wandle

The River Wandle runs for 9 miles, from Croydon and Carshalton in the south to the Thames in the north. The river has a strong flow, making it perfect for water-powered factories. At one time there were nearly 100 mills along the banks. Unfortunately these mills dumped their waste into the river, and it became badly polluted. Alan Suttee (right), a local campaigner, describes the problem: "In the late 1960s the Wandle was officially designated an open sewer. And in the '70s I remember it running red, pink, or blue, depending on what dye they were using in the local tanneries."

Long sections had also become choked with weeds and trash. In the 1990s a small team of local residents, led by Suttee, began to work on clearing the river of debris. "We've pulled out supermarket trolleys, motorbikes, safes, and even guns. You wouldn't believe what's in that river," said Suttee.

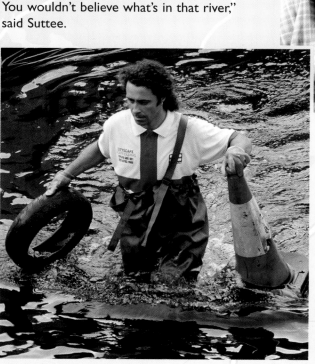

Many of the volunteers were fishermen who knew that the river had once been famous for its trout fishing. They were first rewarded in 2002 when a fly fisherman caught a two-pound brown trout in the river. It is believed to be the first trout caught in London in 70 years.

◀ A volunteer removes trash from the river.

Transportation for London

London was home to the world's first underground train system, which opened in 1863. London also has a local system of surface trains. Today more than 3 million passengers use the Underground system (or "Tube," as it is known) every weekday. The network has more than 500 trains and employs more than 12,000 people. The Tube has been expanded greatly from the early days, and this growth is continuing today with work on extending the Jubilee line.

▲ New buses using more ecofriendly fuels are being introduced.

Complementing the Tube system are London's buses. In the past these were criticized as slow and unreliable. Increased bus use is a key goal for those in charge of transportation in London. To encourage this, more buses have been introduced to improve service frequency and bus lanes created to reduce the problem of buses being held up by traffic. Cameras record car drivers who use bus lanes and issue them fines. In late 2005, free bus travel for full-time students under age 16 was introduced as a further incentive. These policies have contributed to a 38 percent increase in bus use between 2000 and 2005, and today there are more than 6,800 buses carrying an estimated 6 million people every weekday.

▲ ▶ Every day, millions of people use the Underground to get around. There are stations dotted everywhere, making it a convenient way of crossing the city.

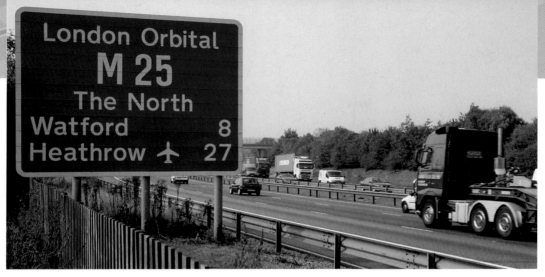

▲ The M25 is the world's largest ring road, completely encircling London. Delays are often so bad that people jokingly call it the world's largest parking lot!

External transportation links

London is linked into a system of eight highways, and once drivers have escaped the London traffic they can head in any direction they choose. London is ringed by the M25 highway, which feeds onto routes in all directions.

London is also well connected to other UK cities (and even some in mainland Europe) through an extensive train network. Engineering work on Eurostar, a high-speed train link from London to the Channel Tunnel and Europe, is expected to finish in 2007. The link is a 67-mile line, with much of the London section passing through deep tunnels. A 2-mile stretch will pass under the Thames at Dartford, then a 12-mile tunnel will lead to St. Pancras

▲ Eurostar trains go from central London to Paris and Brussels.

Station in central London. London is served by four international airports—City, Heathrow, Gatwick, and Stansted—though the last two are actually outside Greater London. Although London's role as a seaport has declined, ships still bring goods to the city from around the world. Most of the seaborne goods destined for London arrive at Tilbury, 19 miles east of the city.

Other (taxi, motorcycle, light rail) 2%
Bicycle 2%
Underground (Tube) 10%
Rail 5%
Car 42%
Bus 18%
Walk 21%

◀ Typical daily journeys in London, and how they are made.

Traffic congestion

Even though the narrow old street plan of central London was not laid out with cars in mind, they still need to find a route through the city. In the past the volume of traffic caused terrible congestion, with whole areas of the city "gridlocked" by lines of traffic at the busiest times of day.

One of the Mayor's main priorities has been to try to ease this congestion, which pollutes the center of the city and causes health problems for London's citizens. Congestion has been tackled in two main ways. The first is through congestion charging (see page 44). The second is by encouraging people to use alternative forms of transportation.

Cycling and walking

The city is trying to encourage more people to bicycle in London because of the health and environmental benefits it brings. Courier companies that need to move packages around the city quickly have found using cyclists as quick or quicker than using motorbikes. This emphasis is in contrast with large numbers of still-developing cities, many of which have terrible pollution problems yet see thousands of people abandoning their bikes for cars. In London, bicycle traffic increased by 67 percent between 2000 and 2005. The number of cyclists was still very small, though, at just 101,000 people using bicycles as their main mode of transportation. Many people are put off cycling by the idea of riding in the aggressive London traffic, which carries a risk of injury.

London is also trying to make it easier for people to walk around the city. Pedestrian routes have been improved; road crossings have been added; and street signs give people directions around central London.

▶ Increasing numbers of bicycle lanes have been created in the hope that more Londoners will get on their bikes.

▲ London's streets still experience bad congestion, even after the introduction of the congestion charge (see page 44).

► Small fold-up bikes such as this man's make it easy to use a combination of trains, buses, and bike.

▼ The use of bicycles leapt after terrorists attacked London's Underground system in July 2005.

CASE STUDY

Sarah Hanratty, cyclist

"It always used to take me at least an hour to get to work with a Tube trip across London," says Sarah Hanratty. Sarah used to leave home at about 7:30 in the morning. "One day I decided to cycle. I really felt like riding but was worried about how long it would take. So I set off at 7:00 a.m. I figured the bike would take at least twice as long as the Tube." The result surprised her: "I actually got to work at 7:30. It had taken me half an hour. After that, I never went on the Tube again."

The congestion charge

In 2002 London became one of the first of the world's major cities to introduce congestion charging. This means drivers pay a fee for entering the busy city center. Planners' goal was to discourage unnecessary journeys, reduce the traffic flow, and increase revenue for the city's government. At the same time as the charge was introduced, the Mayor's office increased the number of city buses, encouraging people to use public transportation rather than their cars.

Transport for London, the body in overall charge of transportation in the city, put forward three main reasons for introducing the charge:

- London had the worst congestion in the UK and among the worst in Europe.
- Drivers in central London spent 50 percent of their time in lines.
- Every weekday morning, the equivalent of 25 busy highway lanes of traffic tried to enter central London.

It was estimated that lost time caused by congestion cost businesses £2 million– £4 million ($3.5–$7 million) every week.

The charging plan works between 7:00 a.m. and 6:30 p.m. from Monday to Friday. With a few exceptions, anyone driving in central London during that time has to pay. At first the cost was £5.00 (around $9.00), in 2005 this increased to £8.00 ($14.00). Drivers can pay online, by phone, or by text message. Cameras photograph vehicles entering the charging area, record their license plates, and check whether they have paid. If not, the computer sends out notice of a fine.

Congestion charging has its critics. People claim that it has worsened traffic outside the charging zone, which has become busier with people parking there to avoid the charge. As a result, many areas outside the charging zone have introduced "resident parking" programs, where local people pay for a permit to park their cars.

▼ Signs painted on the road warn drivers they are entering the congestion-charging zone.

Transport for London

Congestion charging

C

Central ZONE

Mon - Fri
7 am - 6.30 pm

18T

Mon - Fri
Midnight - 7am
9pm - Midnight

Sat
Midnight - 7am
1pm - Midnight

Sun
At any time

Except
permit holders

Controlle
ZONE

▲ The congestion-charging zone is clearly marked.

Anyone without a permit cannot park during the day.

Small businesses based inside the congestion-charging zone have complained bitterly about the effect this fee has had on their businesses, especially if quick deliveries are required. Florists, fishmongers, butchers, and any other business that needs deliveries of fresh produce have suffered a large increase in their operating costs. Many small enterprises that have closed for business since the introduction of the charge have blamed their failure on its costs.

The increase in the number of buses has also been controversial, because the investment in new buses has been expensive. Many critics have complained that the money spent on the buses is wasted—they are overfull during rush hours and mainly empty at other times.

In 2007 the charging zone will be extended west to include the boroughs of Kensington and Chelsea. This proposal has been unpopular with local residents. They argue the original central congestion charging zone was a less residential area and that they are being unfairly targeted.

Culture, leisure, and tourism

London has the greatest concentration of major attractions in Britain. These include four World Heritage Sites—the Palace of Westminster, the Tower of London, Maritime Greenwich, and Kew Gardens—and 238 attractions that are free to enter. London's tour guides boast, "There is nowhere else in the world where you can see so much for so little." London's top visitor attractions range from ancient to modern. These, plus the theaters, restaurants, pubs, and clubs, bring billions of tourist dollars each year to the city. Visitors come from all over the UK and the rest of the world.

▲ A military band marches past the front of Buckingham Palace, the Queen's London home.

The National Gallery

The National Gallery, on Trafalgar Square, is the most popular visitor attraction in the whole city. As with many museums and galleries, entry is free. The National is home to one of the world's greatest collections of Western European art, including works by great artists such as Botticelli, Turner, Cezanne, and van Gogh. The separate National Portrait Gallery is at the back of the National, and it houses pictures of famous and infamous people from Britain's past and present.

▶ Nelson's Column, in Trafalgar Square, with the National Gallery in the background. Trafalgar Square is a popular place for New Year's celebrations and political demonstrations.

Tate Modern

Tate Modern is the UK's national museum of modern art. It makes quite a contrast to the National—instead of being housed in a grand old building, the Tate Modern is in a converted power station beside the River Thames. As well as established artists, the gallery includes exhibitions by new artists. Its cavernous main vault has shown some giant pieces of work, which have gone on to be shown around the world.

▲ The Tate Modern can be reached by footbridge from the north bank of the Thames. The bridge was opened as part of London's millennium celebrations.

▼ The London Eye, a giant ferris wheel, is on the south bank of the Thames. It gives views across the whole of London.

The London Eye

Conceived as an entry in a millennium landmark competition (which it didn't win), the London Eye is now one of the city's visitor attractions. Taller than the Statue of Liberty in New York and Big Ben in London, the Eye is a giant wheel providing views of London. On a clear day, views from the Eye can stretch as far as Windsor Castle, almost 25 miles away. Visitors are carried in one of the Eye's 32 capsules, which have mainly glass walls. At full capacity, the wheel can carry 15,000 people a day.

London's top ten tourist attractions

This list is based on the number of visitors per year:

1. National Gallery
2. British Museum
3. Tate Modern
4. London Eye
5. Natural History Museum
6. Science Museum
7. Tower of London
8. Victoria and Albert Museum
9. National Portrait Gallery
10. National Maritime Museum

The value of tourism

Tourists from overseas are crucial to the city's economy. These visitors fall into two broad groups. First are visitors to the UK who pass through London on their way elsewhere—50 percent of visitors to the UK spend time in London. Second are people who come specifically to see the city, who tend to be there longer.

The financial value of tourism is huge: The industry directly and indirectly brings in approximately £15 billion ($26 billion) per year, or 10 percent of the city's GDP. The benefits of tourism are not only financial, they are also cultural: Tourist income helps to pay for many of the city's historical attractions, museums, and galleries. Overseas visitors buy 30 percent of all theater tickets and make up 50 percent of those going to sites such as the Tower of London. Without them, many attractions would struggle to survive and would not be available for Londoners themselves to enjoy.

Tourism to London is affected by events around the world. Since 2001, fears about terrorism, SARS, and avian flu have had a negative impact on visitor numbers. Economic depression in Japan has meant fewer wealthy visitors from the Far East, and a fall in the value of both the U.S. dollar and the European euro ( ) against the UK pound (£) makes it harder for visitors from abroad to afford to come to London.

The 2012 Olympics is expected to boost the number of visitors. As soon as it was announced that London would host the Games, preparations for the sports stadiums, transportation facilities, and accommodations began. More than 10,000 competitors, their coaches, hundreds of thousands of spectators, television crews, reporters, and others will give a huge, but temporary, boost to London's economy.

▼ Leicester Square is popular with tourists and locals alike. Weekends and evenings see the square filled with revelers.

▲ The White Tower of the Tower of London, one of the top ten tourist attractions in the city, was built by William the Conqueror after he claimed the crown in 1066. It has been used as a royal residence, a barracks, and a prison. Today it is home to the crown jewels and is open to the public.

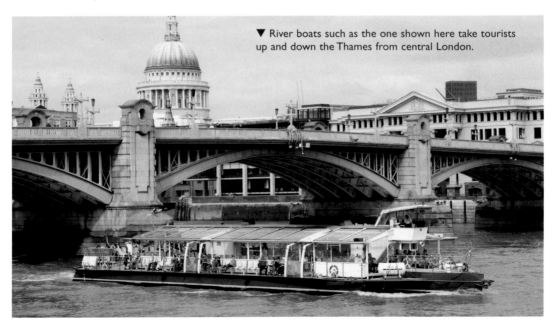

▼ River boats such as the one shown here take tourists up and down the Thames from central London.

Working in the tourist industry

The number of jobs that overseas tourism provides is even more significant than industry's contribution to the city's wealth. It is estimated that a 1 percent increase in overseas tourist numbers results in a 1.28 percent increase in jobs in London. Domestic visitors make a much smaller contribution—they tend to make shorter visits and spend money less freely. A 1 percent increase in tourists from elsewhere in the United Kingdom creates only a 0.34 percent increase in jobs.

Increases in tourist numbers create jobs for waiters, tour guides, and hotel workers, but many more people work in spinoff industries. For example:

- Tourism creates jobs in restaurants, and 22 percent of Britain's restaurants are in London.
- Many tourists like to travel in one of London's traditional black cabs, and there are 21,000 black cabs registered in Greater London. And of course these cabs must be serviced, filled with fuel, and kept clean, all of which provides more work.
- London's theaters are popular with tourists—overseas visitors buy 30 percent of tickets, creating work for theater staff and actors.

▲ Open-topped tourist buses are a popular way to see the city. The buses the tour companies use are often old London buses that have been modified.

◄ The entrance to the expensive Ritz Hotel in Piccadilly, an upmarket area of central London. There are a large number of five-star hotels in London, catering to wealthy visitors. Most of the hotels include prestigious restaurants, providing work for large numbers of highly skilled chefs and waiters.

Leisure and sports

Many of the attractions that bring tourists to London—such as museums, art galleries, and restaurants—are also popular with local people. London is a relatively young city, in that 47 percent of the population are between 16 and 44 years old, compared with 40 percent for the United Kingdom as a whole. Younger people tend to use their leisure time in a more active way, and going out in the city is popular.

Many Londoners also spend their leisure time taking part in sports. There are local soccer and rugby leagues, swimming clubs, cricket contests, and many other team sports. People also enjoy more individual activities such as skateboarding, rock climbing, in-line skating, bicycle racing, and running.

London's successful bid to host the 2012 Olympics means that large new sporting facilities will be built on the site of the Games, Hackney Marshes, to the east of the city. The marshes had been a very large area of informal sports grounds used by thousands of people every weekend. Once the Olympic site has been developed there should be world-class sporting facilities available for the local

▲ Skateboarding among the modernist architecture along the south bank of the Thames is popular.

residents to use. The new Wembley Stadium in northwest London was opened in 2006, replacing the old building, which was demolished in 2000. The UK national government has already proposed making it part of a bid for the 2018 soccer World Cup.

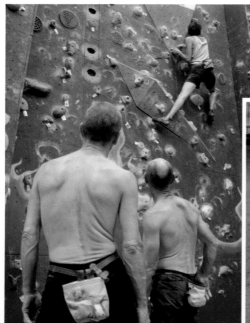

◄ Climbing enthusiasts using an artificial climbing wall in Mile End. There are no large natural climbing areas in the London region.

▼ Soccer is one of the most popular sports. There are many soccer fields throughout the city.

The London environment

A third of London is made up of green space, so most Londoners are rarely far from a park or garden. But the environment is about more than simply trees, flowers, and plants, although these are important. The quality of life for people who live in the city is also linked to the types of buildings they live in and are surrounded by, and to air quality and noise levels.

▲ London's parks and green areas provide a refuge for the city's wildlife as well as for its people.

Five key issues

The Mayor's office coordinates environmental policies for London. There are five major areas of concern for London's environmental planners:

1. Air quality and pollution
The congestion charge is intended to improve air quality by reducing traffic. London is also pioneering the use of hydrogen and fuel-cell power (see page 53).

2. Ambient noise
Ambient noise is the background noise that people hear, mainly from vehicles, such as car traffic and landing aircraft (a particularly

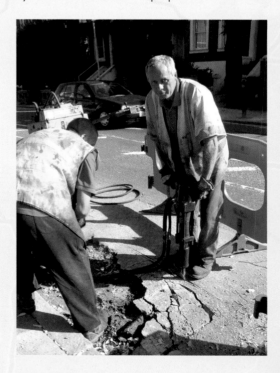

▶ Reducing the amount of noise in London—for example, noise from building work or road repairs—is one of the goals of the city's planners.

acute problem in Hounslow, the area of west London under the Heathrow Airport flight path). One of the goals of introducing hydrogen power to London is to reduce ambient noise: Hydrogen-powered vehicles are almost silent.

3. Biodiversity

Biodiversity is the range of different animals and plants that live in an area. London is home to more than 1,500 species of plants and 300 types of birds, among other animals. In London biodiversity is helped by making sure that wildlife habitats are not lost, and that more open spaces are created. These include London's rivers, allotments (cultivated plots), parks, and gardens.

4. Energy

Use of fossil fuels such as gasoline causes pollution and is unsustainable, because these fuels will one day run out. London therefore needs to use renewable energy sources wherever possible and to be as energy-efficient as it can. Hydrogen-powered vehicles are almost emission-free, so they do not harm the environment. In 2002 the London Hydrogen Partnership

▼ Ecofriendly cars such as the one below help to lower carbon emissions, making the city greener, quieter, and a better place to live.

was launched. Its goal is to help introduce hydrogen power to the city wherever possible. From 2004 to 2006, Transport for London tested three hydrogen-powered buses (see picture on page 40) with the intention of introducing more if the trial was successful. These are a start, but the city needs to do far more in the future if it is to be truly sustainable.

▼ The Mayor's office environmental plan aims to improve the quality of life for all Londoners.

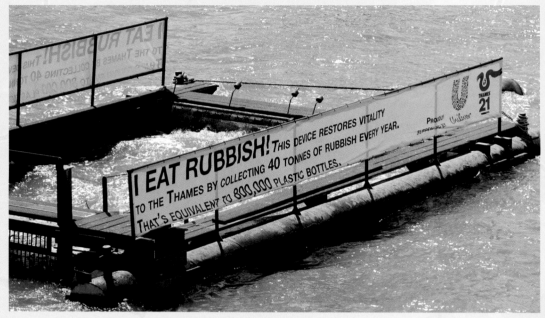

▲ This machine collects surface debris on the Thames as the tide flows through it.

5. Waste

The city's inhabitants generate vast mountains of waste every day, which has to be disposed of. For instance, 177,000 metric tons of litter are dropped every year, costing £100 million ($174 million) in street cleaning. Many Londoners (44 percent) see litter reduction as a priority for improving the quality of London's environment.

In an effort to reduce the amount of waste they generate, Londoners are being encouraged to recycle more. Things are improving: In 2001–02 London's household recycling rate was 9.3 percent, but this rose to 13.2 percent in 2003–04. The city still has a long way to go, though: The United Kingdom's national average for the same year was 17.7 percent, and even this was far from the national target figure of 25 percent.

▶ Over the last 10 years, increasing numbers of Londoners have been taking part in recycling programs run by their local councils.

▲ Affordable offices created by using freight containers in Poplar, east London. The cost of offices can deter many businesses from locating in London.

Architecture

Many exciting new buildings have been built in London in the last few years, including the Swiss Re Tower (page 10), Portcullis House (left), the Lloyd's Building (page 32), and the new City Hall (page 37). London now has an Architecture and Urbanism Unit, headed by the internationally famous architect Richard Rogers. Its goal is to create or improve 100 public spaces in the city by 2010, making the physical environment of the city more pleasant for its inhabitants.

◄ Portcullis House, in Westminster, contains the offices of Members of Parliament.

The London of tomorrow

What might the London of the future be like? One of the main influences on this will be the Mayor's strategies for the city. These have already begun to have a significant effect on, for example, traffic—which is probably the most visible result of the forward planning. The introduction of the congestion charge showed that London, through the Mayor's office, is not afraid to adopt radical solutions to solve its problems.

The London Plan

The city plans to develop as "an exemplary, sustainable world city," in the words of the Mayor, based on three key elements:
* Strong, diverse long-term economic growth.
* Social inclusion, to give all Londoners the opportunity to share in future success.
* Key improvements in London's environment and use of resources.

The Mayor's office has developed the "London Plan" to meet these criteria. It targets areas such as housing, employment, transportation, and the environment. One of the key elements is the promise to build 30,000 new homes in London every year for 15 years, half of which are to be affordable for people on lower incomes. In a survey of Londoners in 2004, 52 percent of people said that one of the worst things about living in the city was the cost of living. A major part of this is the cost of housing: 93 percent of people think that housing in London is too expensive. More affordable homes would improve the economic situation of many Londoners.

In such a large city it is difficult to please everyone, and every element of the London Plan has had its critics. But the plan has been approved by the national UK government and is likely to form the basis of London's future development.

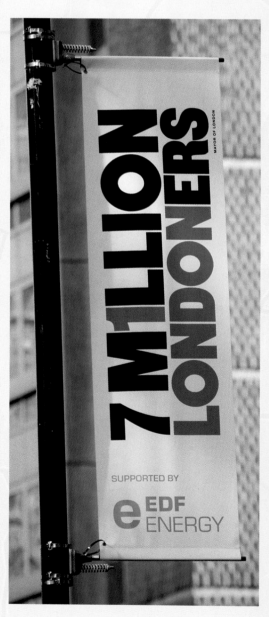

▶ Although London is a diverse city of more than 7 million people, the city's population have an identity and common cause as Londoners.

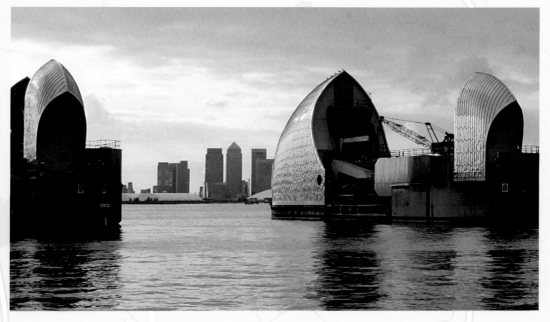

▲ London's Thames Flood Barrier is designed to prevent flooding of the city by regulating the flow of tidal water.

The Thames Flood Barrier

Janine Walker works for the Environment Agency at the Thames Flood Barrier. There, in the Learning Centre, she works with schools and other groups to explain the risk of flooding to London and the role the barrier plays in preventing it. The barrier was opened in 1984 and has been used many times to prevent flooding in the city. London is especially vulnerable, due to a combination of climate change causing rising sea levels, and a natural sinking of land in London and the southeast corner of England. The Thames Barrier was built to cope with tidal levels predicted through 2030. After this point the level of protection provided will decline year by year due to climate change and sea level rise. A new project called Project 2100 is now looking to the future, but as Janine says, "A new barrier is not the answer. We need to think about the way we use space in the city and about our own behavior. We teach about recycling, respect for nature and the river. People will need to understand these issues to help London create a more sustainable future."

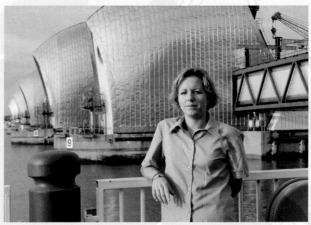

Glossary

allotment A small plot of land in an urban setting generally used for growing food crops.

bond trading The buying and selling of bonds to profit from short-term fluctuations in the market. A bond is a certificate of debt on which the issuer promises to pay the holder interest.

brownfield site An abandoned, often contaminated site that could be used for redevelopment.

Commonwealth A voluntary organization of 53 countries, most of which were at one time governed by the United Kingdom.

convenience food A prepared food that needs only to be heated up before it can be served.

direct action An action by members of the public, such as a strike, boycott, or demonstration, that is meant to quickly atract attention and influence the government.

European Union (EU) An organization of 25 European countries that act together on some economic, political, and social issues.

economic depression A period of time when unemployment is high and people have little money to spend.

ethnic Relating to a group of people who have a shared culture and homeland.

fast food Food that is sold ready to eat and served to the customer soon after it has been ordered. Burgers and pizza are typical examples of fast food.

GDP Gross domestic product, the total value of goods produced and services provided in a country during one year.

infrastructure The physical things that a modern country needs to run efficiently, such as roads, railroads, airports, and power stations.

National Insurance The UK system in which everyone pays a proportion of their salary to the government, which in turn provides health care and pensions for citizens.

nutritious Full of nutrients, chemicals the body needs in order to stay healthy.

obesity The condition of being so overweight that it is bad for one's health.

plague A fast-spreading disease that affects a large proportion of the population.

public housing Housing provided by the government, which is available at a low rent to people who would otherwise find it hard to afford a similar home.

redevelop To improve a rundown area by repairing its buildings and making better use of any vacant land.

regeneration A process in which an area of substandard buildings is replaced with new structures meant to improve residential and business conditions; also called renewal or urban renewal.

retail sector The part of the economy having to do with selling goods to the general public.

semidetached house A house that is joined only to one other.

suburb A residential area on the edge of a large town or city.

sustainability The capacity of a lifestyle to preserve the world for future generations. For example, making sure that trees that are cut down are replaced and avoiding fuels that damage the world's climate are sustainable actions.

United Kingdom (UK) A shortened form of the official name of the British state since 1921: the United Kingdom of Great Britain and Northern Ireland.

urbanization The process by which a population becomes more concentrated into towns or cities.

Further information

Useful Web sites:

City Lifestyle Explorer
http://ceroi.net/cle/
An interactive site that allows visitors to decide how to live in the city then see the impact of their decisions on the city environment.

City of London
http://www.cityoflondon.gov.uk/Corporation
The official site of the Corporation of London and the City; a good source of information about London's economy.

London
http://www.london.gov.uk/
The official Web site of the Mayor of London, the London Assembly, and the Greater London Authority, with a variety of useful snippets about living in London.

Transport for London
http://www.tfl.gov.uk/tfl/
Information about the congestion charge, London's experiments with hydrogen power, the Tube, buses, bicycling in the city, and many other topics.

Visit London
http://na.visitlondon.com/
Plenty of information on London's attractions from the city's official tourism organization; an especially interesting site for those who have never visited the city.

Books to read:

Bailey, Jacqui. *The Story of London: From Roman River to Capital City*. London: A&C Black, 2000.
A quick whiz through London's key events and historical figures.

Chester, Robert, and Nicholas Awde. *London: An Illustrated History*. New York, Hippocrene Books, 2003.
A concise account of the city through time.

Clements, Gillian. *The Great Fire of London*. London: Franklin Watts, 2002.
A lively look at one of the key elements London's history.

Deary, Terry. *Horrible Histories: Loathsome London*. London: Scholastic Hippo, 2005.
A collection of fascinating facts about the history of London.

Hughes, Martin, et al. *London*. 4th ed. Victoria, Australia: Lonely Planet, 2004.
A fact-filled, illustrated travel guide to the city.

Paton Walsh, Jill. *Fireweed*. New York: Farrar, Strauss & Giroux, 1988.
A novel about two runaway teens who refuse to be evacuated from London in the Second World War and then struggle to survive the Blitz of 1940.

Selvon, Sam. *The Lonely Londoners*. White Plains, N.Y.: Longman, 2001.
A much-praised account of what it was like to be a West Indian arriving in London in the 1950s.

Index